How to save your marriage:

5 keys to having the best marriage

Shelly J. Cooper

Table of contents

INTRODUCTION

There are solutions to your issues even if you think your marriage is failing. There are highs and lows in every marriage. However, if you're reading this, yours has likely been down for some time. You might have been going through something extremely stressful lately, such as a new job, having a baby, or having to take care of an elderly parent. Alternately, it's possible that you're fighting over money, that someone cheated, or that your sexual life has ended.

Several different situations have the potential to send a relationship spiraling downward.
One thing is certain when a marriage begins to falter: The needs of the relationship begin to take precedence over those of each partner. That can make it nearly impossible to overcome difficult circumstances.
Additionally, you might feel as though you're always talking past each other rather than being on the same page.
Is that a sign that a divorce is in order? Necessarily not. There are ways to work through your issues and feel closer again, even if you and your partner seem to have seriously drifted apart. According to experts, all you need to do is be willing to put in the effort. Find out if your marriage can survive and what important steps you can take to get back on track in this guide.
How to know if your marriage can be saved. Marriage is a big investment, so it can be hard to tell if it's time to part ways.
In the beginning, examine your shared history honestly. Has your relationship been good overall, aside from your current circumstance? It is normal to go through periods of good and bad times; therefore, if you have recently experienced a difficult time, it is worthwhile to attempt to overcome it.
It can also be helpful to think about how your divorce would affect people outside of your marriage, like your children, extended family, and even

close friends. It is not only acceptable but also necessary to work on your marriage for these stakeholders. Strong families and communities are the results of strong marriages.

Last but not least, consider the possibility that you have been duped into thinking that the grass is always greener on the other side. Problems tend to follow you if you don't address them.

If you have a problem that is causing your current relationship to struggle, such as lying about your spending or becoming jealous for no real reason, it will probably come up in your new relationship as well. Many people fall into the trap of thinking that getting together with a different partner can make them happy.

CHAPTER 1: HOW TO SAVE YOUR MARRIAGE

The Easy Part Is Deciding That You Want to Save Your MarriageNow is the time for you both to put in the effort to resolve your issues and rekindle your connection. The following steps may be of assistance.

Take action right away if you feel like things are getting really bad and want to fix them! It is simple for struggling couples to become involved in the game of "you go first."However, you are increasing the likelihood that absolutely nothing will alter if you wait on your spouse.

Take a look at yourself.

It can be tempting to place all of the blame on your partner. He is the only one who works all the time!)However, people, it takes two to tango. Be sincere about how you might be contributing to the issue as well, rather than focusing too much on what your partner is doing wrong. It's easier to ask your partner to do the same when you can suggest ways that you can get better.

Yes, your feelings and point of view are important; however, talk less and listen more. But you won't ever be able to understand where your spouse is coming from if you only focus on yourself all the time. Therefore, listen to them without worrying about what you'll say next. You can respond once you are certain that you understand exactly what they are trying to say and where they are coming from.

Check your tone.

Calling someone by their name or speaking in a condescending or mean manner immediately puts your partner on the defensive, which can lead to their shutting down. So, even when you're angry, try to be respectful when you talk. By doing this, you demonstrate to your partner that you care enough about them and the relationship to sift through what you say.

Stop talking bad things about yourself. Even if you pretend that everything is fine on the outside, it's easy to get into the habit of criticizing your spouse internally. Your feelings and actions are influenced by your negative thoughts."You'll be better able to effect change once you see yourselves as equals."

Even when you don't feel like it, show kindness. Even small acts of kindness can make a big difference, especially when you and your partner are already close to breaking point.

Therefore, exert more effort. Just for fun, pick up your spouse's favorite ice cream on the way home from work, and say thank you to them when they make the bed or move your dinner plate to the sink. Your partner's behavior will change as well when you express gratitude and kindness.

Reach a stage where you and your partner are unable to come to an agreement or are unsure of the next steps. Avoid the urge to seek guidance from family or friends.

They will have a bias."Integrate an impartial third party, such as a marriage counselor, if you and your partner require assistance navigating.

Be patient.

If a problem is bad enough to make you think about divorce, it won't go away right away. Even if you and your partner are giving it your all, changing harmful communication habits or patterns takes time. Avoid looking for a quick fix. I usually ask couples to commit for at least a year, sometimes even two."It might appear to be forever. However, you both agreed that forever would be yours, right?

CHAPTER 2: COMMUNICATION

Communication is crucial in a marriage. If we asked you what makes a marriage happy, you might say love, commitment, and so on. However, how frequently do we discuss the significance of marriage communication? Let's do that right now!

Five Reasons Why Communication Is Crucial Even if two people spend time together, that does not mean they communicate effectively. To keep a happy marriage and maintain a strong bond, effective communication is essential. The five reasons to improve your communication skills are as follows:

Keeps interest alive If you don't know what the other person is dealing with personally or what is going on in their life, you may gradually lose interest in each other's life.
A relationship can become strained as a result of this lack of interest. Talk about everything to keep your marriage interesting. It enhances your empathy and mutual comprehension.

Get to know each other better

By talking to each other frequently, you can get to know each other better and strengthen your bond. It becomes harder to misunderstand one another when you understand what each is going through. Additionally, it will contribute to a greater sense of mutual support and marital contentment.

Positive marital satisfaction

Improved communication leads to improved marital satisfaction. Open communication reduces disagreements and fosters respect and trust. Couples who can communicate effectively are more likely to have happy and peaceful relationships.
Increased trust, kindness, and respect Communication are two-way. You can't expect to get everything if you don't give something back. Give and

receive constructive criticism. Be completely honest when discussing issues. It will aid in strengthening the relationship's trust and connection.

Better connection

Regularly discussing one's relationship or life outside of marriage enhances connection. It is a means of communicating one's feelings to another.
There is no way to emphasize enough how important communication is in a marriage. Any marriage must be successful. There will be fewer miscommunications and a more complete relationship as a result of effective communication.

CHAPTER 3: THE IMPORTANCE OF SEXUAL INTIMACY IN MARRIAGE

In a marriage, sexual intimacy is crucial to the strength and unity of the couple; However, sexual intimacy goes far beyond just having sex. The genuine closeness, support, and companionship you share with your partner make up the intimacy you share with them.

Sexual intimacy also involves feeling at ease with one another by being who you are and talking about your feelings, desires, and thoughts to one another.

Although sex plays a significant role in sexual intimacy, it is neither the only factor nor the primary variable. If it were, then any two people who have a sexual encounter with each other would automatically have sexual intimacy; however, this is not the case. You will not have sexual intimacy even if you are in love. Despite their love, many couples lack the necessary intimacy. It takes work and the desire of both partners to prioritize a satisfying and high-quality relationship to achieve true and lasting sexual intimacy.

For a happy and healthy marriage, we will go over some of the reasons why you and your partner should explore and improve your sexual intimacy.

Sexual intimacy contributes to emotional and physical well-being. Although studies have shown that married people are not always happier, married people do tend to have better health if their relationship is healthy and fulfilling.

If you have sexual intimacy in your marriage, you will be better able to support one another during times of stress or major life changes.

If you and your spouse struggle to agree on or get along in other areas,

sexual intimacy can help your marriage.
During turbulent times or times when the relationship is under strain, for some couples, sexual intimacy is what keeps the marriage together.
Sexual intimacy positively boosts self-esteem. Your own beliefs about yourself and your worth must be the source of your self-esteem; however, it certainly helps when your partner is supportive and proud of you and your achievements.
Intimacy sexually will assist you in other aspects of your life. Having a strong, intimate relationship with your partner will improve your career, parenting skills, and friendships.

CHAPTER 4: TRUST

A difficult relationship is one in which there is a lack of trust. A marriage or relationship can't flourish if trust is lacking. When it comes to starting and keeping a happy marriage, trust is a must. One of the most important aspects of a relationship and a crucial component of any lifetime commitment is mutual trust. The quality of your relationship will decline if you lack trust.
What is the significance of trust to you?

Trust is essential to a healthy relationship and contributes significantly to your happiness as a whole. You will feel safe, secure, and supported if you trust your spouse. Knowing that you are making a lifetime commitment to someone you can trust and confide in is critical because marriage is a lifetime commitment.

Why is your spouse so concerned about trust?

Because he or she needs to feel safe, happy and supported in your relationship, trust is just as important for your spouse as it is for you. Because the Sacrament of Marriage is about creating a union that will last a lifetime, you and your partner need to have trust in one another so that you can support one another at every stage.

A relationship that suffers from a lack of trust or a breach of trust is extremely challenging. Additionally, it hurts a relationship as a whole. Spouses can become irate, suspicious, and watchful of one another after a trust breach. However, if you and the other person are willing to work together to restore trust, it is possible to reestablish trust and repair breaches of trust.

However, if distrust persists for an extended period, it may cause irreparable harm to a relationship or marriage. It can be difficult for a person to trust their spouse if they have been in a previous relationship or their family has broken trust in them.

In these circumstances, it is essential to discuss your previous interactions with your spouse to assist him or her in comprehending your difficulty and gaining your trust.

A lack of confidence, a sense of inadequacy within oneself, or a general lack of security can also be the root of trust issues. It might be hard for you to believe that your partner only cares about you and is committed to you. In many relationships, doubts and suspicions are common, and fear may be the root cause.

It is essential to discuss your worries with your partner for them to comprehend you and assist you in reducing some of them.

Your spouse may become frustrated and believe it is impossible to earn your trust, and they may even give up trying to earn it as a result of unspoken fears that manifest as doubts and suspicions. If you don't talk about your doubts and worries, they can fester inside of you.

When you talk about your worries, it may become clear to you that you have been worrying too much. You may be able to reduce your feelings and worries and, as a result, increase your level of trust.

During your marriage, it is essential to listen to and discuss your partner openly and honestly regularly.

How to build and keep trust There are numerous ways to build and keep trust with your spouse. Being open, honest, and transparent with your spouse about

your feelings, thoughts, and actions is one of the most important things you can do.
Being consistent, dependable, and dependable is another way to build trust in your marriage. Being on time or taking care of your spouse's errands are easy ways to demonstrate to them that you are there for them and that they can rely on you.
Like everything else, trust needs to be nurtured for it to flourish. To keep it healthy, it needs constant care and attention. Understanding that trust is one of your marriage's essential components is essential to a long-term commitment that is supportive and healthy.
It is necessary to trust; It is difficult to maintain a healthy marriage relationship without it.
Although the term is frequently used, few people take the time to define it.
The confidence or belief you have in another person is called trust. You form a mental image of that person based on that belief. They either reinforce your initial positive perception or instill a negative one based on your actions. Before you get married, your ability to trust in marriage was established in your relationship, and it should continue to grow after you say "I do."
In a healthy marriage, the following are key trust areas:
1. First and foremost, believe in our teamwork.

The phrase "Forsaking all others" is used in many wedding ceremonies. When you consider that vow, you will realize that it signifies that you and your spouse became a family on the day of your marriage and are TEAM #1. You moved beyond ME to WE! This means prioritizing your marriage. Yes, over oneself, as well as over children and friends and family.

2. I have faith in your faithfulness.

A sign of marital faithfulness is trusting your spouse to only share their physical self with you. Being faithful extends beyond your intimate relationship.

Additionally, it includes being trustworthy and open with whomever:

You're talking about your hopes, dreams, struggles, and objectives.

Your time is used.

You use your money (as well as the amount of debt you have).

3. Trust that you won't try to control or harm me on purpose.

For a marriage to be healthy, there needs to be a sense of safety and security. Be deliberate about taking care of, loving, and respecting one another even when normal conflict occurs.

Choose phrases that educate rather than hurt your partner.

4. Believe that you love me for who I am, not what I can give you.

Your partner needs to know that they are loved for who they are inside, not for how they look on the outside. The certainty that you would choose your spouse again despite any physical or financial changes strengthens your relationship.

5. Put your faith in the fact that we will turn to one another, not the other.

There will be ups and downs, sadness, and hurts in marriage. Leaning on one another during difficult times helps to lighten the load.

In a healthy, trusting marriage, a sense of security comes from knowing your partner has your back.

When you extend your hand to your spouse and they extend their hand back to you, there is no greater feeling.

Now that we've talked about how to trust in a marriage, it's important to look at yourself and the things that made you trust in the first place. The interactions you have with friends, family, and coworkers shape your perception of trust.

Sadly, you may have been betrayed and disappointed in previous relationships, including those with friends and family.

You might want to think about the following questions if you want to heal past wounds and build trust in your marriage:

How have my previous relationships, friends, and family damaged my trust?

Have I turned my past betrayals against my partner?

Is there a reason I should not trust my spouse?

You can now begin to cross that chasm and onto a brighter, more trusting marital relationship by beginning to move past those wounds

CHAPTER 5: HOW TO GET A CLEARER PICTURE OF YOUR PARTNER

When we communicate or respond to people with whom we have a relationship, how often do we pay attention to our automatic thinking and actions? We all want to understand our partner so that our relationship can be made even better.

When couples' conflicts and stress are primarily caused by misunderstandings, it becomes crucial for all couples to learn how to be more empathetic to one another.

Meaning of being able to understand your partner means knowing what they mean and what they want without asking. It is an unconscious understanding of one's partner's thoughts and behavior patterns.

Do You Understand Your Partner? When we communicate or respond to people with whom we are in a relationship, how often do we pay attention to our automatic thoughts and actions? We all want to understand our

partner so that our relationship can be made even better.
When couples' conflicts and stress are primarily caused by misunderstandings, it becomes crucial for all couples to learn how to be more empathetic to one another.
Meaning of being able to understand your partner means knowing what they mean and what they want without asking. It is an unconscious understanding of one's partner's thoughts and behavior patterns.
If you've learned to understand your partner, there will be fewer misunderstandings and miscommunications. Even if they are unable to precisely say what they want to say, you will be able to get what they want to say.
If you have taken the time to get to know each other better, your partner's intentions and responses will be revealed to you by just one action, expression, or word.
Why is it important to understand your partner? If the couple has a good understanding of each other and what they expect from each other, their marriage can continue to be healthy and happy.
Couples who lack interpersonal understanding are more likely to get into arguments as a result of misperceptions and incorrect assumptions about one another. A happier and healthier marriage would result from fewer disagreements and a deeper comprehension of one another.

Understanding one's partner is essential to a healthy relationship, according to research. It includes being aware of each other's personal histories, differing marital expectations, and traumatic past experiences.
To form a bond, partners need to feel understood by one another. Their partner makes them feel important, heard, and seen. Additionally, this contributes to an overall increase in marital contentment for both partners.

15 steps to understanding your partner

Understanding your partner often involves romance and chemistry that cannot be explained. But understanding is a skill that can be learned over time. You will have no trouble comprehending your partner's point of view if you are a willing and receptive partner.
It takes some time and careful consideration to learn to understand your partner. Try the steps below and see how beautifully your relationship changes:
1. Understanding yourself first is essential. You must first comprehend your feelings, intentions, and biases. Together, these influence how you perceive everything and everyone in your environment.

After removing your bias from the circumstance, you will be in a better position to evaluate your partner's actions and feelings once you are familiar with yourself. It will also help you understand your partner better because you will be able to draw parallels between your actions and theirs.

2. Using "I statements" I statements are a useful tool and habit that can teach you how to understand your partner. Sentences that begin with "you" are intended to accuse your partner, such as "you are mean."

Without using words like "blame" or "accusations," "I statements" or sentences that start with "i" convey your experience and feelings. Your partner will not feel trapped and become defensive as a result of these statements.

According to research, "I statements" are useful tools for conflict resolution and encourage people to remain open to understanding each other's points of view.

3. Make it a priority to realize that understanding your partner or spouse is neither innate nor a binary choice. If you keep the right attitude, you can learn this skill over time.

Make it a priority for you to understand your partner because this is the only way you will ever truly understand them. Instead of waiting for things to work out on their own, you need to actively work toward understanding your partner.

4. Pay attention to body language cues. Did you catch the shrug? Did you catch that scowl? Did you catch them exhaling deeply? Understanding your partner better can benefit greatly from understanding these cues.

A person's physical expressions and body language tell a lot about how they feel in response to certain situations, words, or actions. You will acquire a subconscious understanding of your partner's responses and thoughts if you begin to read their body language.

You might recognize a pattern in their behavior or their true feelings about particular things. You'll learn how to better understand your partner every day from these observations.

5. Ask them about their childhood. Our childhood has a significant impact on our personality. It influences a person's personality and helps them understand their surroundings.

Understanding your partner's past is necessary for understanding them, as they may be willing to share important details about their early years that have shaped them today.

You can better comprehend their responses and motivations by asking them questions or recalling things they have said about the past. You can tell if their outburst or isolation is caused by a traumatic childhood experience.

6. Show your appreciation by showing your partner how much you appreciate them. It will be easier to learn to understand your partner if they keep

their guard around you so you can understand their true feelings, motives, and impulses.

According to research, expressing gratitude improves relationship satisfaction. Additionally, when people are content in their relationships, they are more at ease letting go of their guard.

They are more likely to open up to you about themselves and not try to hide their feelings in front of you if you show them how much you love and appreciate them. By making them feel accepted and at ease, compliments can demonstrate that you value them.

7. Find out how they communicate. Depending on their culture, personality, and experiences, each person has a unique communication style. Some people communicate through indirect means, while others use words to express exactly how they feel.

Some people find it awkward to talk about themselves, so they may show how they feel by acting or gesturing. Take note of the distinctive combination of communication strategies your partner employs to enhance understanding between you as husband and wife.

8. Take a step back. Fighting is not communicating. Every couple has disagreements and fights; However, if you don't take the right approach, these can be harmful. Leaving a fight can sometimes help you better understand your partner's point of view.

Take a deep breath and move on rather than making accusations at each other. Give yourself a chance to think about what your partner said and did. You might gain a better understanding of one another by reflecting on things.

9. Accept mistakes and follies. Being open and honest with your partner is the only way to understand each other. Accepting your mistakes and taking responsibility for your actions, which will influence your partner's behavior toward you, is a big part of this.

Your partner will feel safe in your presence if you are open and accountable. They will open up more easily because they will feel less judged. Giving your partner a chance to understand you is necessary for them to learn how to understand you.

10. Get to know their loved ones. A person's loved ones have a significant impact not only on how they shape them but also on how they respond to situations. Get to know them because they are a window into your partner's personality.

Allow your relationship with your partner's loved ones to grow in trust. They might be able to tell you things about your partner that you didn't know, or they might just show what kind of people your partner values.

11. Ask them about their wants and needs. Guesswork can be fun and frustrating at the same time. Therefore, rather than trying to guess what your partner requires, ask them.

Who they are and what they value informs people's needs and desires.
As a result, you can gain a better understanding of your partner by asking them directly about their requirements. It will demonstrate your concern for them while also revealing your partner's identity.
12. Be there for them. Crucial aspects of a person's personality and coping mechanisms are revealed during trying times. Therefore, when your partner is going through a difficult time, take the time to show them your sincere support.
Your partner will be able to confide in you and trust you during difficult times if you support them. You will be able to better comprehend your partner as a result of this.
13. You won't be able to understand your partner unless they are open with you. Respect their boundaries. Respecting their boundaries is a significant factor in ensuring this. Your partner is much more likely to become hostile or cold toward you if you violate their boundaries.
As a means of protecting their space, they may have raised their defenses around you, making it extremely difficult to understand them.
Try to respect your partner's personal space and boundaries. You can earn your partner's trust and get them to open up to you at their own pace by doing this.
14. Be presently Tired of work? Are you lost in thought? Be present when

you are with your partner because doing so will allow you to notice things about them. If you don't pay attention, you might miss how they are feeling or a change in them.

You can learn how to get to know your partner better by being present, which will also show them how important you are to them. They will be more receptive, allowing you to better understand them.

15. Consult a specialist Sometimes, it's best to work with a specialist. You can talk to a therapist if you have trouble understanding your partner. They might be able to provide you with useful tools to address your particular issue and make it easier for you and your partner to communicate.

Final thoughts Although it may require additional effort to comprehend your partner's thoughts, actions, and feelings, implementing the aforementioned strategies can strengthen your relationship.

You must foster an atmosphere of openness and actively seek to learn more about your partner. Take control of the situation rather than waiting for an intuitive understanding to emerge.

Take the time to continue learning about your partner to facilitate healing and growth in your relationship and learn how to understand them.

CHAPTER 6: RESPECT'S SIGNIFICANCE IN MARRIAGE

Respect is crucial in a marriage. Perhaps more than any other factor. Moreover, I will explain why.

The best way to express respect is to truly appreciate another person. Respect is not just a feeling; it is an action. It is a declaration of someone else's value. By how we treat another person, we demonstrate respect.

And it's not hard to tell when someone treats another person with respect or disrespect.

Most people believe that showing respect comes from a place of inferiority. When high-ranking officers enter the room, images of soldiers standing at attention or employees praising their boss comes to mind.

However, respect in a happy marriage is different. There are two sides to it. With good reason, the two people in the relationship want and need to be treated with the same respect.

In marriage, respect is shown not because one partner is superior to the other, but rather because each partner acknowledges the value of the other.

Respect for each other is important in marriage.

Why then? Why is respect for one another so important to a happy marriage?

Four reasons include:

I. The fear of being different is eliminated through mutual respect. Let me elaborate. Each of you comes to the relationship in your marriage as an individual. You have your personality traits, abilities, quirks, interests, and previous experiences. Respect for one another demonstrates appreciation for one another, despite differences.

The differences your spouse brings to the relationship are valued by your respect for them. Respect for one another makes it possible for each person to be themselves without fear of being devalued or judged unfairly.

II. Respect for one another maintains healthy boundaries in the relationship. Proper boundaries are reinforced in even the healthiest marriages.

When you treat your spouse with respect and appreciation, you are aware of their specific needs. For instance, I'm the kind of person who needs some alone time every day to recharge.

Even though she does not have the same need, my wife respects that and knows when to give me some space. Even if it's in jest, it's important to my wife that we don't call each other names because sometimes things can get out of hand or be misinterpreted.

Even though I was raised to playfully call people names, I try to respect that.

Respect for one another gives us the strength to stick to these limits.

III. When you disagree, mutual respect forces you to "check your jersey. It's easy to believe that your spouse is working against you in this team effort called marriage when things are heated. Respect does not eliminate the possibility of disagreements; Even in the best marriages, they will.

However, you will feel more at ease knowing that you and your spouse are on the same team and working toward the same goal if you regularly practice mutual respect in your marriage. It is easier to see that you are both wearing the same jersey.

IV. The friendship you share with your spouse is bolstered by respect for one another. According to relationship expert John Gottman, intentional friendship in a marriage fosters long-term vitality and connection.

To put it another way, if you and your spouse strengthen your friendship, your marriage will be healthy. Respecting one another cultivates friendship because it demonstrates appreciation and value for one another. Why? because it takes away the worry of being vulnerable. Because I can be most vulnerable with my wife, she is my best friend. Without mutual respect, that can't happen.

But hold on—there's more!

Bonus explanation of why respect for one another is important in marriage!

Children must be taught to respect each other. As parents, you and your partner undoubtedly want your children to be respectful adults. Watching how their parents treat one another is a child's primary source of respect.

My wife and I have two daughters. I think it's important for them to know how husbands and wives should treat one another: with love, care, and respect. We hope they can recognize that in us. Teaching children to be respectful in a marriage requires mutual respect.

Respect is important in your marriage.

Find ways to show your spouse how much you appreciate them, despite their differences, and do so every day. Show that you value your spouse by what you do. You'll become better teammates, parents, and friends.

CONCLUSION

Final Thoughts on Saving Your Marriage There are a lot of things you can do. Although the exit door may appear to be the simplest option, if you and your partner decide to work toward reconciliation, it is never too late to form a mutually beneficial partnership; However, if there is any kind of physical or emotional abuse, it might be better to leave than to continue causing harm by staying.

www.ingramcontent.com/pod-product-compliance
Lightning Source LLC
LaVergne TN
LVHW052114160826
845678LV00015B/3545

* 9 7 9 8 3 5 9 0 8 3 3 1 7 *